How to Knit Socks
Three Methods Made Easy™

HOUSE of
WHITE
BIRCHES

PUBLISHERS
SINCE 1947

2

Table of Contents

Double-Pointed Needles page 5

4 Three Methods for Knitting Socks

Basic Sock on Double-Pointed Needles
Basic Sock on Two Circular Needles
Basic Sock on One Circular Needle

18 Flip-Flop Socks

21 Eyelet Rib Socks

24 Grain Stitch Socks

28 Tied Cable Ribs Socks

32 Bright Slip-Stitch Socks

36 Harris Tweed Rib Socks

40 Baby Lace Socks

General Information, **43**
Photo Index, **48**

*Two Circular Needles
page 9*

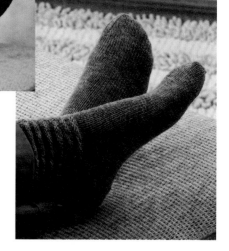

*Flip-Flop Socks,
page 18*

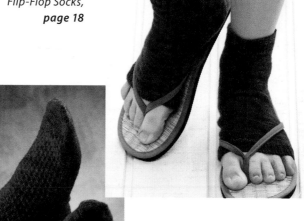

*Grain Stitch Socks,
page 24*

*Harris Tweed Rib Socks,
page 36*

Introduction

Socks are a never-ending source of pleasure for knitters. They are small, portable and functional. Furthermore, they offer an unlimited opportunity to play with texture, color and all those elements that keep our fingers and our minds happily engaged.

For perhaps hundreds of years, people have been knitting socks using double-pointed needles. In recent years, other sock-knitting techniques have become popular as knitters look for alternative ways to knit small-circumference tubes in the round. In this book, you'll learn three different methods of knitting socks in the round:

- Using double-pointed needles.
- Using two circular needles.
- Using one long circular needle, sometimes called the Magic Loop.

These instructions are written for working one sock at a time. Using the two circular needles or Magic Loop method, it is possible to work two socks at the same time using separate balls of yarn. While this has the advantage of getting both socks completed at the same time, for purposes of learning a new technique we'll just concentrate on working one sock at a time.

Start with the basic sock in sport weight yarn to learn the basics of sock knitting. Take time to understand this type of sock construction—the way the different parts of the sock relate to one another—and you'll find it easy to use these methods in other socks.

The construction of all the socks in this book is the same:

- Start with a cuff and/or leg which is worked in rib or another type of stitch which will hold the sock up.

- Work back and forth on a heel flap, while the instep (top-of-the-foot) stitches are left unworked.
- Turn the heel using short-row shaping on the heel flap stitches.
- Pick up stitches along the sides of the heel flap, and begin working in the round once more.
- Decrease two stitches every other round, placing the decreases where the instep joins the side of the heel flap, to create a gusset.
- Work even in rounds until the foot is the desired length, minus the length needed for toe shaping.
- Decrease four stitches every other round (and then every round) at the sides of the foot, to create toe shaping.
- Arrange top-of-foot stitches and bottom-of-foot stitches on parallel needles so they may be grafted together.
- Graft toe stitches for a seamless finish.

If this terminology sounds confusing, don't worry. You'll know what it means by the time you complete the basic sock.

No matter which method you decide to use to knit your socks, you'll find the step-by-step directions and photographs make your sock-knitting experience educational and enjoyable.

Three Methods for Knitting Socks

- **Double-Pointed Needles**
- **Two Circular Needles**
- **One Long Circular Needle**

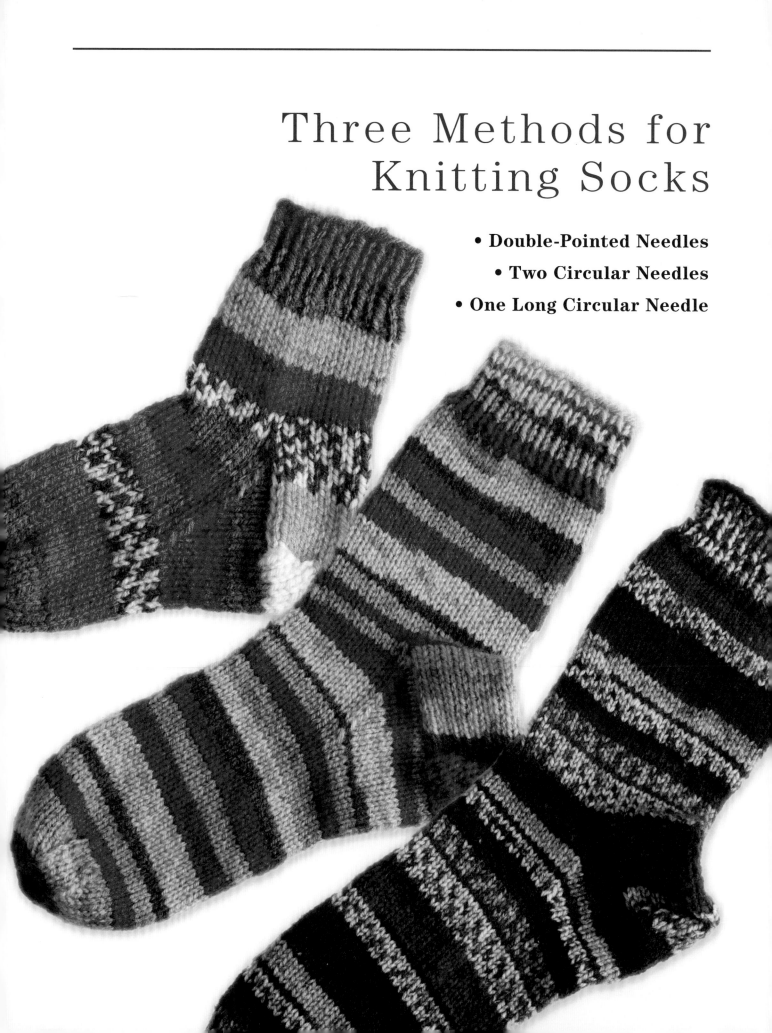

Basic Sock on Double-Pointed Needles

To help you learn these new methods, we included tips and explanatory information in italics. These sections are also indented to set them apart. If you already know how to knit socks in this method, you can follow the regular text only. Read the indented, italic section if you want more explanation than is given in the basic instructions.

The three socks in the instructional section are knit in self-striping yarn. If you haven't tried knitting with these wonderful sock yarns, now is the time to start. All the yarns used in this book are available from AnniesAttic.com.

Sizes
Child's (Woman's, Man's) Instructions are given for smallest size, with larger sizes in parentheses. When only 1 number is given, it applies to all sizes.

Finished Measurements
Foot Circumference: 5½ (6½, 8) inches
Foot Length: 6 (9¼, 11) inches

Materials
- DK weight acrylic yarn (147 yds/50g per ball) 1 ball for child's size, 2 balls for woman's or man's size—3 balls needed for longer or taller sock
- Size 3 (3.25mm) double-pointed needles or size needed to obtain gauge: set of 4 or 5
- Stitch markers
- Tapestry needle

Gauge
12 sts and 17 rnds = 2 inches in St st.
To save time, take time to check gauge.

Project Note: With this method, stitches waiting to be knit are arranged on 3 or 4 needles. A 4th or 5th needle serves as the active needle. These instructions are written as if you are using a set of 5 needles, with changes for a set of 4 needles in brackets.

Cuff
Cast on 32 (40, 48) sts loosely. Arrange sts for working in the rnd.

Arrange stitches so that ¼ of the stitches are on each of 4 needles [approximately ⅓ of the stitches are on each of 3 needles]. You will be knitting with the 5th [4th] needle.

Join, being careful not to twist sts. Knit 1 rnd.

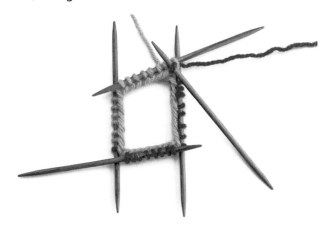

House of White Birches, Berne, Indiana 46711   DRGnetwork.com

Hold the needles so that they form a square [a triangle]. Making sure that the cast-on edge does not twist around the needles, insert the free needle into the first stitch you cast on. Using the working yarn attached to the last stitch cast on, knit this stitch. Continue knitting all the stitches on the first needle. When the stitches on the first needle have been knit, use that needle to knit the stitches on the next needle. Continue using the newly empty needle to knit the stitches off the next needle, until you have reached the end of the round.

Change to K1, P1 Rib and work until sock measures 1¼ (1½, 1½) inches. Change to St st and work even until sock measures 2¾ (5, 6½) inches from beg.

Heel

Knit 16 (20, 24). Turn. Arrange sts for working heel, with 16 (20, 24) sts on heel flap and 16 (20, 24) sts on instep. Work back and forth in rows on heel sts only.

Knit the first half of the stitches onto a single needle. The remaining half of the stitches will be evenly divided onto 2 needles, and will become the instep (top of the foot). Ignore them while you work back and forth on the heel flap. Turn the work so that the purl side of the heel flap stitches faces you.

Heel Flap Stitches

Instep Stitches

Row 1 (WS): Sl 1 as to purl, purl across. Turn.

Continue to work back and forth on 2 double-pointed needles until the heel flap and heel turning are complete.

Row 2 (RS): Sl 1 as to knit, knit across. Turn.

Rep [Rows 1 and 2] 7 (9, 11) times, ending with a RS row.

Turning heel

Note: Sl 1 as to knit on RS rows and sl 1 as to purl on WS rows.

Row 1 (WS): P10 (12, 14), p2tog, p1. Turn, leaving rem sts unworked.

Row 2 (RS): Sl 1, k5, ssk, k1, turn.

Row 3: Sl 1, p6, p2tog, p1, turn.

Row 4: Sl 1, k7, ssk, k1, turn.

For Child's Size Only
Row 5: Sl 1, p8, p2tog, turn.

Row 6: Sl 1, k8, ssk—10 sts.

Continue with Gusset.

For Woman's & Man's Sizes Only
Row 5: Sl 1, p8, p2tog, p1, turn.

Row 6: Sl 1, k9, ssk, k1, turn.

For Woman's Size Only
Row 7: Sl 1, p10, p2tog, turn.

Row 8: Sl 1, k10, ssk—12 sts.

Continue with Gusset.

For Man's Size Only
Row 7: Sl 1, p10, p2tog, p1, turn.

Row 8: Sl 1, k11, ssk, k1, turn.

Row 9: Sl 1, p12, p2tog, p1, turn.

Row 10: Sl 1, k12, ssk—14 sts.

Continue with Gusset.

Gusset

Rnd 1: With RS of heel facing you, pick up and knit 9 (11, 13) sts along right edge of heel flap; k16 (20, 24) instep sts; pick up and knit 9 (11, 13) sts along left edge of heel flap, knit first 5 (6, 7) sts of heel—44 (54, 64) sts.

Continuing without turning, on first needle, pick up and knit stitches along right edge of heel flap (as sock is worn); on 2nd and 3rd needles [2nd needle], knit across all the instep stitches; on 4th [3rd] needle, pick up and knit stitches along left edge of heel flap, knit next half of stitches from the bottom of the heel. Place remaining half of bottom-of-heel stitches onto first needle. The beginning of the round is now at the bottom of the foot. Continue working in the round.

Rnd 2: On right edge of heel flap, knit to 3 sts from end of gusset sts, k2tog, k1; knit instep sts; on left edge of heel flap, k1, ssk, knit rem sts in rnd—42 (52, 62) sts.

On first needle, knit to last 3 stitches, k2tog, k1; on 2nd and 3rd needles [2nd needle], knit; on 4th [3rd] needle, k1, k2tog, knit to end of needle.

Rnd 3: Knit.

Rep [Rnds 2 and 3] 5 (6, 7) times—32 (40, 48) sts.

Foot

Work even until foot measures 4½ (7½, 9) inches from back of heel, or about 1½ (1¾, 2) inches shorter than desired length of sock.

Toe shaping

Rnd 1: Knit to 3 sts before right edge of foot, k2tog, k1; k1, ssk, knit to 3 sts before left edge of foot, k2tog, k1; k1, ssk, knit to end of in rnd—28 (36, 44) sts.

On first needle, knit to last 3 stitches, k2tog, k1; working on 5 needles: on 2nd needle, k1, ssk, knit to end, on 3rd needle, knit to last 3 stitches, k2tog, k1; [working on 4 needles: on 2nd needle, k1, ssk, knit to last 3 stitches, k2tog, k1]; on last needle, k1, ssk, knit to end.

Rnd 2: Knit.

Rep [Rnds 1 and 2] 2 (4, 5) times—20 (20, 24) sts.

Work [Rnd 1 only] 2 (2, 3) times—12 sts.

Finishing

Arrange sts so that 6 sts for the top of the foot are on 1 needle and 6 sts for the bottom of the foot are on a 2nd needle (Photo A).

> *To arrange the stitches for grafting, knit the 3 stitches from the first needle to the last needle. If necessary, slip all the instep stitches onto 1 needle. You should now have half the stitches on each of 2 needles, with the working end of the yarn coming from the first stitch on the back needle, ready to graft.*

With tapestry needle, graft toe tog (Photo B).

Weave in all ends (Photo C). ❖

Photo B

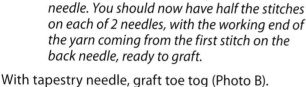

Photo C

Photo A

Sample knit with Sassy Stripes acrylic DK weight yarn #6980 Rave from Moda Dea.

Basic Sock on Two Circular Needles

To help you learn these new methods, we included tips and explanatory information in italics. These sections are also indented to set them apart. If you already know how to knit socks in this method, you can follow the regular text only. Read the indented, italic section if you want more explanation than is given in the basic instructions.

Sizes
Child's (Woman's, Man's) Instructions are given for smallest size, with larger sizes in parentheses. When only 1 number is given, it applies to all sizes.

Finished Measurements
Foot Circumference: 5½ (6½, 8) inches
Foot Length: 6 (9¼, 11) inches

Materials
- DK weight acrylic yarn (147 yds/50g per ball) 1 ball for child's size, 2 balls for woman's or man's size—3 balls needed for longer or taller sock
- Size 3 (3.25mm) needles or size needed to obtain gauge: 2 circular
- Stitch markers
- Tapestry needle

Gauge
12 sts and 17 rnds = 2 inches in St st.
To save time, take time to check gauge.

Project Note: Choose 2 circular needles of the same diameter, with a length of at least 24 inches. You may want to use different types or colors of needles so that you can easily tell one from another. Throughout the entire sock, stitches are knit from the end of 1 needle onto the other end of the same needle, unless the instructions say otherwise.

Cuff
Cast on 32 (40, 48) sts loosely. Arrange sts for working in the rnd.

> *Arrange stitches so that half of the stitches are on 1 needle and the other half are on the 2nd needle. Slide the stitches onto the center cable of each needle. Fold cast-on in the center so that the wrong sides of the cast-ons are together and the needles are parallel. Hold needles so that the working end of the yarn is coming from the rear needle.*

Join, being careful not to twist sts. Knit 1 rnd.

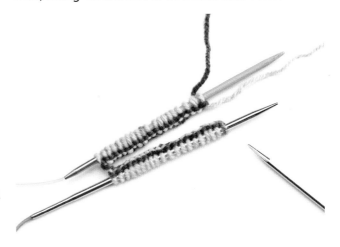

Ensure that the stitches are not twisted around the needle. Holding both needles parallel with the stitches cast on last in the back, *slide the stitches on the front needle to the right tip of the front needle. Ignore the back needle and its stitches for a moment. Bring the other tip of the front needle around in position to knit. You now have a "left-hand" and "right-hand" needle on the front. Insert tip of the right-hand needle into the first stitch on the left-hand needle.

Using the working yarn attached to the last stitch worked, knit this stitch. Continue knitting all the stitches on the front needle, from the left to the right. When those front stitches have been knit, slide the just-completed stitches into the center of the cable. Turn the work so that the "back" needle becomes the "front" needle. Repeat from *, knitting all stitches across this needle. You have completed 1 round when you have knitted all the stitches on both needles.

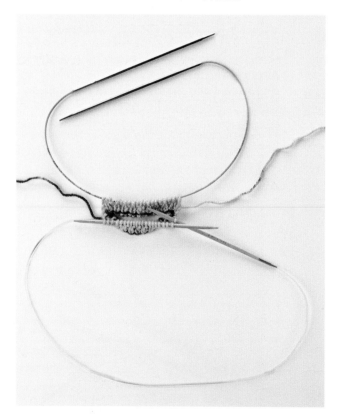

Change to K1, P1 Rib and work until sock measures 1¼ (1½, 1½) inches. Change to St st and work even until sock measures 2¾ (5, 6½) inches from beg.

Heel

Knit 16 (20, 24). Turn. Arrange sts for working heel, with 16 (20, 24) sts on heel flap and 16 (20, 24) sts on instep. Work back and forth in rows on heel sts only.

Knit 20 (24, 28) stitches and turn. Your front needle now holds the instep stitches. Ignore the instep stitches while you work back and forth on the heel flap stitches currently on the back needle. Do not pull on the cable to reset the stitches.

Row 1 (WS): Sl 1 as to purl, purl across. Turn.

Using the free end of the back needle, sl 1, purl across the stitches on the back needle. Do not pull on the cable to reset the stitches. Turn.

Row 2 (RS): Sl 1 as to knit, knit across. Turn.

Using the free end of the front needle, slip 1, knit across the stitches on the front needle. Do not pull on the cable to reset the stitches. Turn.

Rep [Rows 1 and 2] 7 (9, 11) times, ending with a RS row.

Turning heel

Note: Sl 1 as to knit on RS rows and sl 1 as to purl on WS rows.

Row 1 (WS): P10 (12, 14), p2tog, p1. Turn, leaving rem sts unworked.

Row 2 (RS): Sl 1, k5, ssk, k1, turn.

Row 3: Sl 1, p6, p2tog, p1, turn.

Row 4: Sl 1, k7, ssk, k1, turn.

For Child's Size Only
Row 5: Sl 1, p8, p2tog, turn.

Row 6: Sl 1, k8, ssk—10 sts.

Continue with Gusset.

For Woman's & Man's Size Only
Row 5: Sl 1, p8, p2tog, p1, turn.

Row 6: Sl 1, k9, ssk, k1, turn.

For Woman's Size Only
Row 7: Sl 1, p10, p2tog, turn.

Row 8: Sl 1, k10, ssk—12 sts.

Continue with Gusset.

For Man's Size Only
Row 7: Sl 1, p10, p2tog, p1, turn.

Row 8: Sl 1, k11, ssk, k1, turn.

Row 9: Sl 1, p12, p2tog, p1, turn.

Row 10: Sl 1, k12, ssk—14 sts.

Continue with Gusset.

Gusset

Rnd 1: With RS of heel facing you, pick up and knit 9 (11, 13) sts along right edge of heel flap; knit 16 (20, 24) instep sts; pick up and knit 9 (11, 13) sts along left edge of heel flap, knit first 5 (6, 7) sts of heel—44 (54, 64) sts.

Picking up stitches along the sides of the heel flap and starting the gusset is a bit uncomfortable on the first round, but becomes easier.

With right side of heel facing, and using the right-hand tip of front needle, pick up and knit stitches along right edge of heel flap (as sock is worn), place marker, knit half the instep stitches from the instep needle.

Slide the stitches you just knit to the center of the cable, turn. Slide the stitches on the needle holding the remaining instep stitches to the tip of needle in preparation to knit. Using other tip of instep needle, knit across remaining instep stitches, place marker, then pick up knit stitches along left side of heel flap (as sock is worn). Turn sock 90 degrees so that the remaining stitches of the heel are facing you.

Using the right-hand tip of the same needle, knit half of the bottom-of-heel stitches from the tip of first needle, slide stitches to center of cable, turn.

You now have half the stitches on 1 needle and half on the other needle, with markers separating the instep stitches from the bottom-of-foot stitches. The beginning of the round is now at the bottom of the foot. Continue working in the round.

Rnd 2: On right edge of heel flap, knit to 3 sts from end of gusset sts, k2tog, k1; knit instep sts; on left edge of heel flap, k1, ssk, knit rem sts in rnd—42 (52, 62) sts.

The front needle is now holding the right side of the sock and the back needle is holding the left side of the sock. On front needle, knit to 3 stitches from marker, k2tog, k1, knit to end of needle, slide stitches to center of cable, turn. On front needle, knit to marker, k1, ssk, knit to end of needle, slide stitches to center of cable, turn.

Rnd 3: Knit.

Rep [Rnds 2 and 3] 5 (6, 7) times—32 (40, 48) sts.

Foot

Work even until foot measures 4½ (7½, 9) inches from back of heel, or about 1½ (1¾, 2) inches shorter than desired length of sock.

Toe shaping

Rnd 1: Knit to 3 sts before right edge of foot, k2tog, k1; k1, ssk, knit to 3 sts before left edge of foot, k2tog, k1; k1, ssk, knit to end of in rnd—28 (36, 44) sts.

The markers indicate the edges of the foot. Therefore, *on the front needle, knit to 3 stitches from marker, k2tog, k1, slip marker; k1, ssk, knit to end of needle, slide stitches to center of cable, turn.

Repeat from * once more.

Rnd 2: Knit.

Rep [Rnds 1 and 2] 2 (4, 5) times—20 (20, 24) sts.

Work [Rnd 1 only] 2 (2, 3) times—12 sts.

Finishing

Arrange sts so that 6 sts for the top of the foot are on 1 needle and 6 sts for the bottom of the foot are on a 2nd needle.

To arrange the stitches for grafting, using right-hand tip of back needle, knit half of the stitches from front needle, then tug on tip of needle so that these stitches slip down next to the stitches already on the same needle. Turn. Slip first stitches from front needle to back needle so that there are the same number of stitches on the front and back needles. You should now have 6 stitches on each needle, with the working end of the yarn coming from the first stitch on the back needle, ready to graft.

With tapestry needle, graft toe tog. Weave in all ends. ❖

Sample knit with Sassy Stripes acrylic DK weight yarn #6935 Vintage from Moda Dea.

Basic Sock on One Long Circular Needle

To help you learn these new methods, we included tips and explanatory information in italics. These sections are also indented to set them apart. If you already know how to knit socks in this method, you can follow the regular text only. Read the indented, italic section if you want more explanation than is given in the basic instructions.

Sizes
Child's (Woman's, Man's) Instructions are given for smallest size, with larger sizes in parentheses. When only 1 number is given, it applies to all sizes.

Finished Measurements
Foot Circumference: 5½ (6½, 8) inches
Foot Length: 6 (9¼, 11) inches

Materials
- DK weight acrylic yarn (147 yds/50g per ball) 1 ball for child's size, 2 balls for woman's or man's size—3 balls needed for longer or taller sock
- Size 3 (3.25mm) needles or size needed to obtain gauge: 1 long circular
- Stitch markers
- Tapestry needle

Gauge
12 sts and 17 rnds = 2 inches in St st.
To save time, take time to check gauge.

Project Note: This method is often called the "Magic Loop" method. Use a circular needle with a sturdy cable and a length of at least 30 inches. Stitches are knit from 1 end of the needle onto the other end while maintaining a loop of cable between one half of the stitches and the other half.

Cuff
Cast on 32 (40, 48) sts loosely. Arrange sts for working in the rnd.

> *Slide all stitches to the center of the cable. Fold the cable so that there is a sharp bend at the halfway point of the cast-on stitches. Pull the cable between 2 stitches at this point, gently forcing half the stitches onto 1 end of the needle and the other half onto the other end of the needle.*

The resulting loop made by the cable will stay in place throughout all portions of the sock.

Join, being careful not to twist sts. Knit 1 rnd.

*Ensure that the stitches are not twisted around the needle. Holding needle tips parallel and pointing to the right, with the stitches cast on most recently in the back, *pull on the cable so that the front half of the stitches slide to the front tip of the needle. Pull the back tip of the needle to free it for knitting so that the back stitches are on the cable, maintaining a loop on the left side of the sock. Ignore the back stitches for a moment. Bring the free (back) tip of the needle into position to knit. You now have a "left-hand" and "right-hand" needle, and 2 loops between the front and back stitches, 1 on either side. Insert tip of the right-hand needle into the first stitch on the left-hand needle. Using the working yarn attached to the last stitch worked, knit this stitch.*

*Continue knitting all the stitches on the front of the needle, from left to right. When those front stitches have been knit, turn the work so that the "back" stitches become the "front" stitches. Repeat from *, knitting all stitches across this needle. You have completed 1 round when you have knitted across all the stitches on both needles.*

Change to K1, P1 Rib and work until sock measures 1¼ (1½, 1½) inches. Change to St st and work even until sock measures 2¾ (5, 6½) inches from beg.

Heel

Knit 16 (20, 24). Turn. Arrange sts for working heel, with 16 (20, 24) sts on heel flap and 16 (20, 24) sts on instep. Work back and forth in rows on heel sts only.

Knit 20 (24, 28) stitches and turn. The front needle now holds the instep stitches. Ignore the instep stitches while you work back and forth on the heel flap stitches currently on the back needle. Do not pull on the cable to reset the stitches.

Row 1 (WS): Sl 1 as to purl, purl across. Turn.

Using the free tip of the needle, sl 1, purl across the stitches on the back needle. Do not pull on the cable to reset the stitches. Turn.

Row 2 (RS): Sl 1 as to knit, knit across. Turn.

Using the free tip of the needle, sl 1, knit across the stitches on the front needle. Do not pull on the cable to reset the stitches. Turn.

Rep [Rows 1 and 2] 7 (9, 11) times, ending with a RS row.

Turning heel

Note: Sl 1 as to knit on RS rows and sl 1 as to purl on WS rows.

Row 1 (WS): P10 (12, 14), p2tog, p1. Turn, leaving rem sts unworked.

Row 2 (RS): Sl 1 as to knit, k5, ssk, k1, turn.

Row 3: Sl 1, p6, p2tog, p1, turn.

Row 4: Sl 1, k7, ssk, k1, turn.

For Child's Size Only
Row 5: Sl 1, p8, p2tog, turn.

Row 6: Sl 1, k8, ssk—10 sts.

Continue with Gusset.

For Woman's & Man's Size Only
Row 5: Sl 1, p8, p2tog, p1, turn.

Row 6: Sl 1, k9, ssk, k1, turn.

For Woman's Size Only
Row 7: Sl 1, p10, p2tog, turn.

Row 8: Sl 1, k10, ssk—12 sts.

Continue with Gusset.

For Man's Size Only
Row 7: Sl 1, p10, p2tog, p1, turn.

Row 8: Sl 1, k11, ssk, k1, turn.

Row 9: Sl 1, p12, p2tog, p1, turn.

Row 10: Sl 1, k12, ssk—14 sts.

Continue with Gusset.

Gusset

Rnd 1: With RS of heel facing you, pick up and knit 9 (11, 13) sts along right edge of heel flap; knit 16 (20, 24) instep sts; pick up and knit 9 (11, 13) sts along left edge of heel flap, knit first 5 (6, 7) sts of heel—44 (54, 64) sts.

With the right side of heel facing, and using right-hand tip of front needle (the one you just used to knit a RS row of the heel), pick up and knit stitches along right edge of heel flap (as sock is worn), place marker, knit half the instep stitches from the instep needle.

Slide the stitches you just knit to the center of the cable, turn. Maintaining a loop on both sides, knit across remaining instep stitches.

Place marker, then pick up knit stitches along left edge of heel flap (as sock is worn).

Slide all stitches to the center of the cable so the loop disappears. Create 2 new loops as follows: Fold cable at halfway point of bottom of heel [5 (6, 7) stitches from end of needle for Basic Sock]. Fold cable at halfway point of instep and pull to create loop.

Slide first half of heel stitches onto left-hand tip of needle in preparation to knit.

Knit to end of needle, turn. You now have half the stitches on each side of the needle, separated by 1 large loop. The beginning of the round is now at the bottom of the foot.

Continue working in the round.

Rnd 2: On right edge of heel flap, knit to 3 sts from end of gusset sts, k2tog, k1; knit instep sts; on left edge of heel flap, k1, ssk, knit rem sts in rnd—42 (52, 62) sts.

The front half of the needle is now holding the right side of the sock and the back half of the needle is holding the left side of the sock. On front needle, knit to 3 stitches from marker, k2tog, k1, knit to end of needle.

Slide stitches to center of cable, turn. On front needle, knit across, slide stitches to center of cable, turn. On front needle, knit to marker, k1, ssk, knit to end of needle, slide stitches to center of cable, turn.

Rnd 3: Knit.

Rep [Rnds 2 and 3] 5 (6, 7) times—32 (40, 48) sts.

Foot

Work even until foot measures 4½ (7½, 9) inches from back of heel, or about 1½ (1¾, 2) inches shorter than desired length of sock.

Toe shaping

Rnd 1: Knit to 3 sts before right edge of foot, k2tog, k1; k1, ssk, knit to 3 sts before left edge of foot, k2tog, k1; k1, ssk, knit to end of in rnd—28 (36, 44) sts.

The markers indicate the edges of the foot. Therefore, *on the front half of the needle, knit to 3 stitches from marker, k2tog, k1, slip marker; k1, ssk, knit to end of this half of needle, turn. Repeat from * once more.

Slide all stitches onto cable and create 2 new loops by pulling out a loop at each marker. Knit first few stitches of next round so that yarn ends up at marker. You should now have half the stitches on each half of the needle, with the working end of the yarn coming from the first stitch on the back needle, ready to graft.

With tapestry needle, graft toe tog. Weave in all ends. ❖

Rnd 2: Knit.

Rep [Rnds 1 and 2] 2 (4, 5) times—20 (20, 24) sts.

Work [Rnd 1 only] 2 (2, 3) times—12 sts.

Finishing

Arrange sts so that 6 sts for the top of the foot are on 1 needle and 6 sts for the bottom of the foot are on a 2nd needle.

Sample knit with Sassy Stripes acrylic DK weight yarn #6948 Polo from Moda Dea.

Flip-Flop Socks

Design by Edie Eckman

Skill Level

 INTERMEDIATE

Size
Woman's

Finished Measurements
Foot Circumference: 7 inches
Sock Length: 7½ inches

Materials
- Sock weight superwash merino wool/ nylon blend yarn (192 yds/50g per ball): 2 balls purple
- Size 2 (2.75mm) knitting needles or size needed to obtain gauge: double-pointed OR 2 circular OR 1 long circular needle
- Stitch markers
- Tapestry needle

Gauge
16 sts and 22 rnds = 2 inches/5mm St st.
To save time, take time to check gauge.

Pattern Note
Refer to Basic Sock pattern on page 4 for specifics of arranging stitches on needles according to your preferred method of knitting.

Sock

Cuff
Cast on 60 sts loosely.

Arrange sts for working in the rnd. Join, being careful not to twist sts. Work K1, P1 Rib for 1 inch.

Change to St st and work even until sock measures 2½ inches.

Heel
Knit 30 sts. Turn. Arrange sts for working heel, with 30 sts for heel flap and 30 sts for instep. Work next rows back and forth on heel sts only.

Row 1 (WS): Sl 1 as to purl, purl across. Turn.

Row 2 (RS): Sl 1 as to knit, knit across. Turn.

Rep Rows 1 and 2 until heel measures 2¾ inches, ending with a RS row.

Turning heel
Note: Sl 1 as to knit on RS rows and sl 1 as to purl on WS rows.

Row 1 (WS): P17, p2tog, p1. Turn, leaving rem sts unworked.

Row 2 (RS): Sl 1, k5, ssk, k1, turn.

Row 3: Sl 1, p6, p2tog, p1, turn.

Row 4: Sl 1, k7, ssk, k1, turn.

Row 5: Sl 1, p8, p2tog, p1, turn.

Row 6: Sl 1, k9, ssk, k1, turn.

Row 7: Sl 1, p10, p2tog, p1, turn.

Row 8: Sl 1, k11, ssk, k1, turn.

Row 9: Sl 1, p12, p2tog, p1, turn.

Row 10: Sl 1, k13, ssk, k1, turn.

Row 11: Sl 1, p14, p2tog, p1, turn.

Row 12: Sl 1, k15, ssk, k1, turn.

Row 13: Sl 1, p15, p2tog.

Row 14: Sl 1, k14, ssk—16 sts.

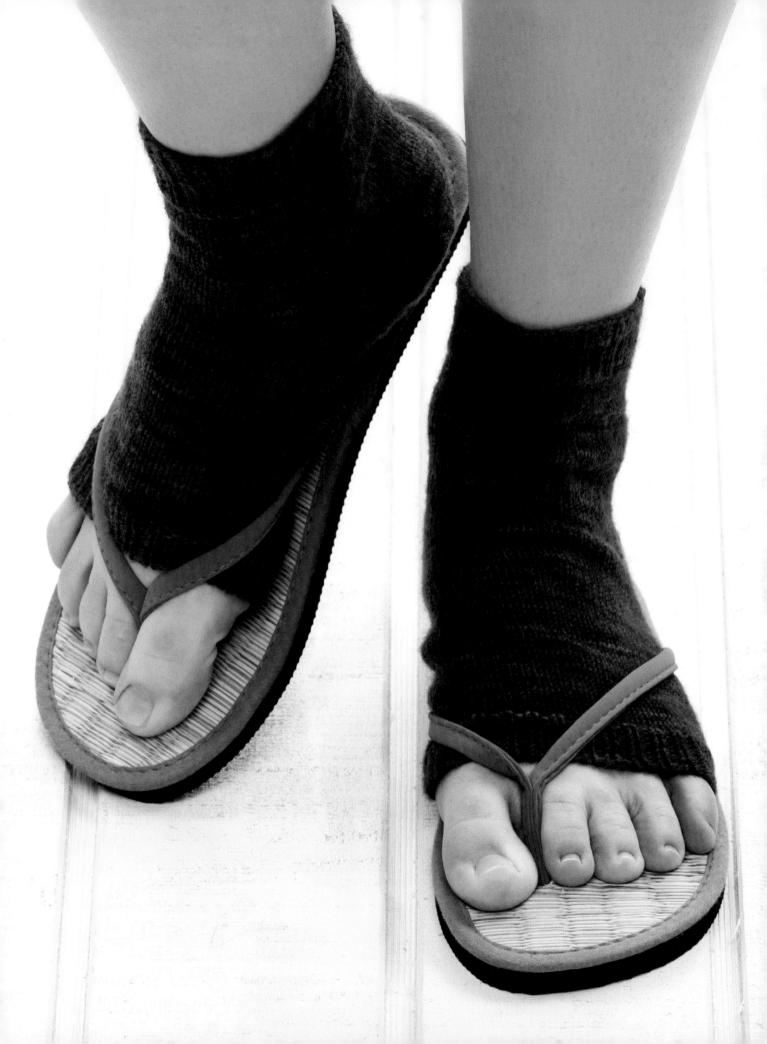

Gusset

Rnd 1: With RS of heel facing you, pick up and knit 16 sts along right edge of heel flap; knit instep sts, pick up and knit 16 sts along left edge of heel flap; knit first 8 sts of heel. Arrange sts for working gusset—78 sts.

Rnd 2: On right edge of heel flap, knit to 3 sts from end of gusset sts, k2tog, k1; knit instep sts; on left edge of heel flap, k1, ssk, knit rem sts in rnd—76 sts rem.

Rnd 3: Knit around.

Rep [Rnds 2 and 3] 8 times—60 sts rem.

Foot

Work even until foot measures 6¾ inches from back of heel, or about ¾ inches shorter than desired length of sock.

Work K1, P1 Rib for ¾ inches.

Bind off. Weave in all ends. ❖

Sample knit with Happy Feet #5 (90 percent superwash merino wool/10 percent nylon) from Plymouth Yarn Co.

Eyelet Rib Socks

Design by Edie Eckman

Skill Level

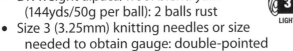 INTERMEDIATE

Size

Woman's

Finished Measurements

Foot Circumference: 6½ inches
Foot Length: 9¼ inches

Materials

- DK weight alpaca/wool blend yarn (144yds/50g per ball): 2 balls rust
- Size 3 (3.25mm) knitting needles or size needed to obtain gauge: double-pointed OR 2 circular OR 1 long circular
- Split-ring stitch markers
- Tapestry needle

3 LIGHT

Gauge

12 sts and 16 rnds = 2 inches in Eyelet Rib pat.
To save time, take time to check gauge.

Special Abbreviation

Make 1 (M1): Inc by inserting tip of LH needle under horizontal strand between st just worked and next st, k1-tbl.

Pattern Stitch

Eyelet Rib (multiple of 5 sts)
Rnd 1: *K2, yo, k2tog, k1; rep from * around.
Rnd 2: Knit around.
Rep Rnds 1 and 2 for Eyelet Rib pat.

Pattern Note

Refer to Basic Sock pattern on page 4 for specifics of arranging stitches on needles according to your preferred method of knitting.

Sock

Cuff

Cast on 45 sts loosely.

Arrange sts for working in the rnd. Join, being careful not to twist sts.

Rnd 1: *K2, p2, k1; rep from * around.

Rep Rnd 1 until sock measures 1½ inches.

Change to Eyelet Rib pat and work even until sock measures 6 inches from beg, ending with Rnd 1 of pat.

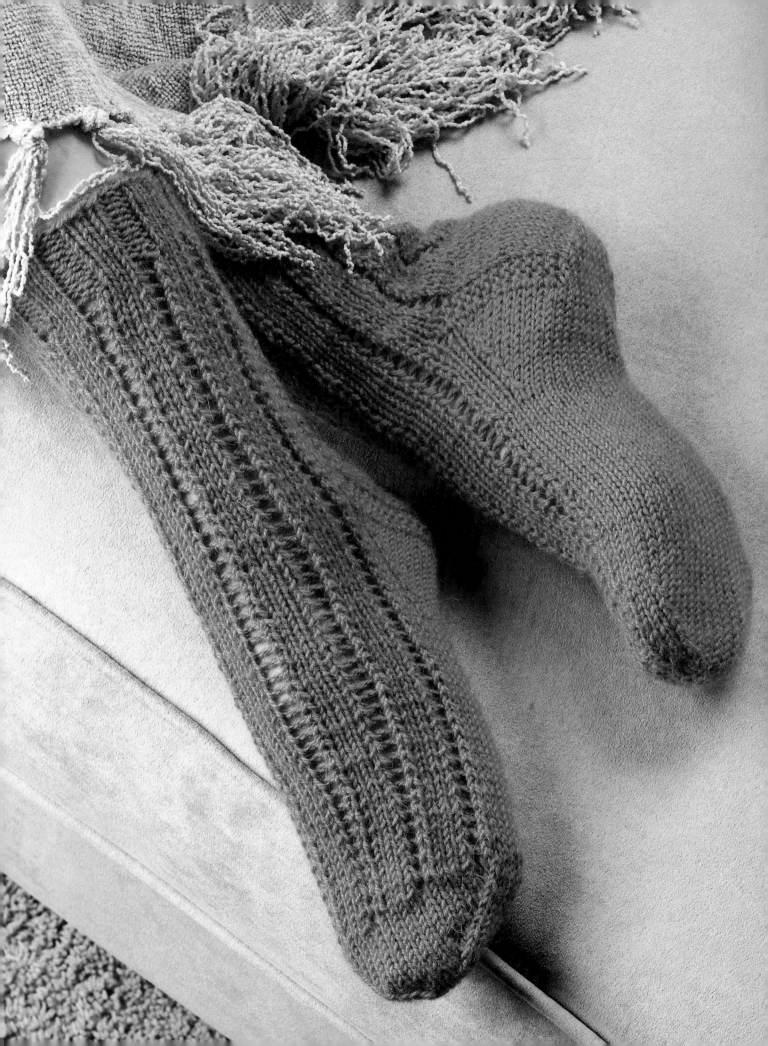

Heel

Slip next 20 sts onto 2 needles (for double-pointed needles method), 1 needle (for 2 circular needles method) or one half of needle (for long circular needle method) for instep. Work back and forth in rows on rem 25 sts for heel flap as follows:

Row 1 (WS): K2, purl to last 2 sts, k2. Turn.

Row 2 (RS): Knit. Turn.

Rep [Rows 1 and 2] 10 times, ending with a RS row.

Turning heel

Note: Sl 1 as to knit on RS rows and sl 1 as to purl on WS rows.

Row 1 (WS): P15, p2tog, p1. Turn, leaving rem sts unworked.

Row 2 (RS): Sl 1, k6, ssk, k1, turn.

Row 3: Sl 1, p7, p2tog, p1, turn.

Row 4: Sl 1, k8, ssk, k1, turn.

Row 5: Sl 1, p9, p2tog, p1, turn.

Row 6: Sl 1, k10, ssk, k1, turn.

Row 7: Sl 1, p11, p2tog, p1, turn.

Row 8: Sl 1, k12, ssk, k1, turn.

Row 9: Sl 1, p13, p2tog, turn.

Row 10: Sl 1, k14, ssk—15 sts.

Gusset

Rnd 1: With RS of heel facing you, pick up and knit 12 sts along right edge of heel flap; work 20 instep sts in established pat; pick up and knit 12 sts along left edge of heel flap, knit first 7 sts of heel, M1. Arrange sts for working gusset—60 sts.

Rnd 2: On right edge of heel flap, knit to 3 sts from end of gusset sts, k2tog, k1; work instep sts in established pat; on left edge of heel flap, k1, ssk, knit to end of rnd—58 sts.

Rnd 3: Knit around.

Rep [Rnds 2 and 3] 7 times—44 sts.

Foot

Work even until foot measures 7½ inches from back of heel, or about 1¾ inches shorter than desired length of sock. Move markers (or move instep sts) so 1 bottom-of-foot st on each side moves to instep sts/needle—22 instep sts and 22 bottom-of-foot sts.

Toe shaping

Rnd 1: Knit to 3 sts before right edge of foot, k2tog, k1; k1, ssk, knit to 3 sts before left edge of foot, k2tog, k1; k1, ssk, knit to end of rnd—40 sts.

Rnd 2: Knit.

Rep [Rnds 1 and 2] 4 times—24 sts.

Work [Rnd 1 only] 3 times—12 sts.

Knit first 3 sts of next rnd and arrange sts so that 6 sts for the top of the foot are on 1 needle and 6 sts for the bottom of the foot are on a 2nd needle.

Finishing

With tapestry needle, graft toe tog. Weave in all ends. ❖

Sample knit with Ultra Alpaca Light #4226 pumpkin puree (50 percent super fine alpaca/50 percent wool) from Berroco.

Grain Stitch Socks

Design by Edie Eckman

Skill Level

 INTERMEDIATE

Size
Woman's

Finished Measurements
Foot Circumference: 7 inches
Foot Length: 9½ inches

Materials
- Sock weight superwash merino wool/ nylon blend yarn (192 yds/50g per ball): 2 balls red
- Size 2 (2.75mm) knitting needles or size needed to obtain gauge: double-pointed OR 2 circular OR 1 long circular
- Stitch markers
- Tapestry needle

Gauge
16 sts and 22 rnds = 2 inches in Grain St pat.
To save time, take time to check gauge.

Pattern Stitch
Grain Stitch (multiple of 4 sts)
Rnds 1 and 3: Knit.
Rnd 2: *Yo, k2, pass yo over k2, k2; rep from * around.
Rnd 4: *K2, yo, k2, pass yo over k2; rep from * around.
Rep Rnds 1–4 for Grain St pat.

Pattern Note
Refer to Basic Sock pattern on page 4 for specifics of arranging stitches on needles according to your preferred method of knitting.

Sock

Cuff
Cast on 60 sts loosely.

Arrange sts for working in the rnd. Join, being careful not to twist. Work K1, P1 Rib for 1¼ inches.

Change to Grain St pat and work even until sock measures 5 inches, ending with Rnd 2 or 4 of pat.

Heel
K30 sts. Turn. Arrange sts for working heel, with 30 sts for heel flap and 30 sts for instep. Work next rows back and forth on heel sts only.

Row 1 (WS): Sl 1 as to purl, purl across. Turn.

Row 2 (RS): Sl 1 as to knit, knit across. Turn.

Rep Rows 1 and 2 until heel measures 2¾ inches, ending with a RS row.

Turning heel
Note: Sl 1 as to knit on RS rows and sl 1 as to purl on WS rows.

Row 1 (WS): P17, p2tog, p1. Turn, leaving rem sts unworked.

Row 2 (RS): Sl 1, k5, ssk, k1. Turn, leaving rem sts unworked.

Row 3: Sl 1, p6, p2tog, p1, turn.

Row 4: Sl 1, k7, ssk, k1, turn.

Row 5: Sl 1, p8, p2tog, p1, turn.

Row 6: Sl 1, k9, ssk, k1, turn.

Row 7: Sl 1, p10, p2tog, p1, turn.

Row 8: Sl 1, k11, ssk, k1, turn.

Row 9: Sl 1, p12, p2tog, p1, turn.

Row 10: Sl 1, k13, ssk, k1, turn.

Row 11: Sl 1, p14, p2tog, p1, turn.

Row 12: Sl 1, k15, ssk, k1, turn.

Row 13: Sl 1, p15, p2tog.

Row 14: Sl 1, k14, ssk—16 sts.

Gusset

Rnd 1: With RS of heel facing you, pick up and knit 16 sts along right edge of heel flap; work 30 instep sts in established Grain St pat; pick up and knit 16 sts along left edge of heel flap, knit first 8 sts of heel. Arrange sts for working gusset—78 sts.

Rnd 2: On right edge of heel flap, knit to 3 sts from end of gusset sts, k2tog, k1; knit instep sts in established pat; on left edge of heel flap, k1, ssk, knit rem sts in rnd—76 sts rem.

Rnd 3: Knit around.

Rep [Rnds 2 and 3] 8 times—60 sts rem.

Foot

Work even until foot measures 7½ inches from back of heel, or about 2 inches shorter than desired length of sock.

Toe shaping

Rnd 1: Knit to 3 sts before right edge of foot, k2tog, k1; k1, ssk, knit to 3 sts before left edge of foot, k2tog, k1; k1, ssk, knit to end of rnd—56 sts.

Rnd 2: Knit around.

Rep [Rnds 1 and 2] 6 times—32 sts.

Rep [Rnd 1] 4 times—16 sts.

Knit first 4 sts of next rnd and arrange sts so that 8 sts for the top of the foot are on 1 needle and 8 sts for the bottom of the foot are on a 2nd needle.

Finishing

With tapestry needle, graft toe tog. Weave in all ends. ❖

Sample knit with Happy Feet #4 (90 percent superwash merino wool/10 percent nylon) from Plymouth Yarn Co.

Tied Cable Ribs Socks

Design by Edie Eckman

Skill Level

 INTERMEDIATE

Size
Woman's

Finished Measurements
Foot Circumference: 6½ inches
Foot Length: 9¼ inches

Materials
- DK weight acrylic/wool blend yarn (150 yds/50g per ball): 2 balls turquoise
- Size 4 (3.5mm) knitting needles or size needed to obtain gauge: double-pointed OR 2 circular OR 1 long circular
- Split-ring stitch markers
- Cable needle
- Tapestry needle

Gauge
12 sts and 16 rnds = 2 inches in St st.

To save time, take time to check gauge.

Pattern Stitch
Tied Cable Rib (multiple of 10 sts)

See chart.

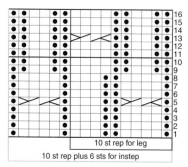

STITCH KEY
☐ Knit
⊡ Purl
⧓ SI 2 sts to cn and hold in back, k2, k2 from cn

10 st rep for leg
10 st rep plus 6 sts for instep

CHART

Pattern Note
Refer to Basic Sock pattern on page 4 for specifics of arranging stitches on needles according to your preferred method of knitting.

Sock

Cuff
Cast on 50 sts loosely. Arrange sts for working in the rnd. Join, being careful not to twist sts.

Work [Rnds 1–16 of Tied Cable Rib pat] twice, then Rnds 1–8 once.

Heel
Using 2 needles (for double-pointed needles method), 1 needle (for 2 circular needles method) or one half of needle (for long circular needle method), work in established pattern over next 26 sts for instep, knit rem sts. Work back and forth in rows on rem 24 sts as follows:

Row 1 (WS): SI 1 as to purl, purl across. Turn.

Row 2 (RS): SI 1 as to knit, knit across. Turn.

Rep [Rows 1 and 2] 11 times, ending with a RS row.

Turning heel
Note: SI 1 as to knit on RS rows and sl 1 as to purl on WS rows.

Row 1 (WS): P14, p2tog, p1. Turn, leaving rem sts unworked.

Row 2 (RS): SI 1, k5, ssk, k1, turn.

Row 3: SI 1, p6, p2tog, p1, turn.

Row 4: SI 1, k7, ssk, k1, turn.

Row 5: SI 1, p8, p2tog, p1, turn.

Row 6: SI 1, k9, ssk, k1, turn.

Row 7: SI 1, p10, p2tog, p1, turn.

Row 8: Sl 1, k11, ssk, k1, turn.

Row 9: Sl 1, p12, p2tog, turn.

Row 10: Sl 1, k12, ssk—14 sts.

Gusset

Rnd 1: With RS of heel facing you, pick up and knit 13 sts along right edge of heel flap; work 26 instep sts in established pat (see chart); pick up and knit 13 sts along left edge of heel flap, knit first 7 sts of heel. Arrange sts for working gusset—66 sts.

Rnd 2: On right edge of heel flap, knit to 3 sts from end of gusset sts, k2tog, k1; work instep sts in established pat; on left edge of heel flap, k1, ssk, knit to end of rnd—64 sts.

Rnd 3: Rep Rnd 2—62 sts.

Rnd 4: Knit.

Rep [Rnds 3 and 4] 7 times—48 sts.

Foot

Work even until foot measures 7¼ inches from back of heel, or about 2 inches shorter than desired length of sock. Move markers (or move instep sts) so 1 instep st on each side moves to bottom-of-foot sts/needle—24 instep sts and 24 bottom-of-foot sts.

Toe shaping

Rnd 1: Knit to 3 sts before right edge of foot, k2tog, k1; k1, ssk, knit to 3 sts before left edge of foot, k2tog, k1; k1, ssk, knit to end of rnd.

Rnd 2: Knit.

Rep [Rnds 1 and 2] 5 times—24 sts.

Work [Rnd 1 only] 3 times—12 sts.

Knit first 3 sts of next rnd and arrange sts so that 6 sts for the top of the foot are on 1 needle and 6 sts for the bottom of the foot are on a 2nd needle.

Finishing

With tapestry needle, graft toe tog. Weave in all ends. ❖

Sample knit with Encore DK #1317 (75 percent acrylic/25 percent wool) from Plymouth Yarn Co.

Bright Slip-Stitch Socks

Design by Edie Eckman

Skill Level

 INTERMEDIATE

Size
Child's medium

Finished Measurements
Foot Circumference: 6 inches
Foot Length: 7½ inches

Materials
- Light worsted weight wool/nylon blend yarn (177 yds/50g per ball): 1 ball each lavender (MC), pink (A) and lime (B)
- Size 2 (2.75mm) knitting needles or size needed to obtain gauge: double-pointed OR 2 circular OR 1 long circular
- Stitch markers
- Tapestry needle

Gauge
16 sts and 20 rnds = 2 inches in St st.
To save time, take time to check gauge.

Pattern Notes
Refer to Basic Sock pattern on page 4 for specifics of arranging stitches on needles according to your preferred method of knitting.

Slip all stitches with yarn on wrong side. Slip stitches as to purl unless otherwise indicated.

Sock

Cuff
With MC, cast on 48 sts loosely.

Arrange sts for working in the rnd. Join, being careful not to twist sts. Work K2, P2 Rib for ¾ inch.

Rnds 1 and 2: With MC, knit around.

Rnd 3: With A, *k3, sl 1 wyib; rep from * around.

Rnd 4: *P3, sl 1 wyib; rep from * around.

Rnd 5: With MC, *k1, sl 1 wyib, k2; rep from * around.

Rnd 6: Knit around.

Rnd 7: With A, *k1, sl 1 wyib, k2; rep from * around.

Rnd 8: *P1, sl 1 wyib, p2; rep from * around.

Rnd 9: With MC, *k3, sl 1 wyib; rep from * around.

Rnd 10: Knit.

Rnds 11 and 12: With A, rep Rnds 3 and 4.

Rnds 13 and 14: With MC, rep Rnds 5 and 6. Cut A.

Rnd 15: Rep Rnd 5.

Rnd 16: WIth MC, knit around.

Work [Rnds 3–16] once, using B instead of A. Cut B.

Heel
K24 sts. Turn. Arrange sts for working heel, with 24 sts for heel flap and 24 sts for instep. Work next rows back and forth on heel sts only.

Row 1 (WS): With MC, purl across. Turn.

Row 2 (RS): With A, sl 1 as to knit, k1, *sl 1, k1; rep from * across.

Row 3: Sl 1, purl to end. Turn.

Row 4: With B, sl 1 as to knit, sl 1, *k1, sl 1; rep from * to last 2 sts, k2. Turn.

Row 5: Sl 1, purl to end.

Rep [Rows 2–5] 5 times, then rep [Rows 2 and 3] once. Cut A and B.

Next row (RS): With MC, *k1, sl 1; rep from * to last 2 sts, k2. Turn.

Turning heel

Note: Sl 1 as to knit on RS rows and sl 1 as to purl on WS rows.

Row 1 (WS): P14, p2tog, p1. Turn, leaving rem sts unworked.

Row 2 (RS): Sl 1, k5, ssk, k1, turn.

Row 3: Sl 1, p6, p2tog, p1, turn.

Row 4: Sl 1, k7, ssk, k1, turn.

Row 5: Sl 1, p8, p2tog, p1, turn.

Row 6: Sl 1, k9, ssk, k1, turn.

Row 7: Sl 1, p10, p2tog, p1, turn.

Row 8: Sl 1, k11, ssk, k1, turn.

Row 9: Sl 1, p12, p2tog, turn.

Row 10: Sl 1, k12, ssk—14 sts.

Gusset

Rnd 1: With MC and RS of heel facing you, pick up and knit 13 sts along right edge of heel flap; knit 24 instep sts; pick up and knit 13 sts along left edge of heel flap, knit first 7 sts of heel. Arrange sts for working gusset—64 sts.

Rnd 2: On right edge of heel flap, knit to 3 sts from end of gusset sts, k2tog, k1; knit across instep sts; on left edge of heel flap, k1, ssk, knit rem sts in rnd—62 sts.

Rnd 3: Knit.

Rep [Rnds 2 and 3] 7 times—48 sts.

Foot

Rnd 1: With A, *sl 1, k1; rep from * around.

Rnds 2–4: Knit around. Cut A.

Rnd 5: With MC, *k1, sl 1; rep from * around.

Rnds 6–8: Knit around.

Rnds 9–12: With B, rep Rnds 1–4. Cut B.

Rnds 13–16: With MC, rep Rnds 5–8.

Rnds 17–20: With A, rep Rnds 1–4. Cut A.

Rnd 21: With MC, rep Rnd 5.

With MC, work even until foot measures 6 inches from back of heel, or about 1½ inches shorter than desired length of sock. Cut MC.

Toe shaping

Rnd 1: With B, *k1, sl 1; rep from * around.

Rnd 2: Knit to 3 sts before right edge of foot, k2tog, k1; on instep, k1, SSK, knit to 3 sts before left edge of foot, k2tog, k1; on left edge of foot, k1, ssk, knit to end of rnd—44 sts.

Rnd 3: Knit around.

Rep [Rnds 2 and 3] 5 times—24 sts.

Rep [Rnd 2] 3 times—12 sts.

Knit first 3 sts of next rnd and arrange sts so that 6 sts for the top of the foot are on 1 needle and 6 sts for the bottom of the foot are on a 2nd needle.

Finishing

With tapestry needle, graft toe tog. Weave in all ends. ❖

Sample knit with Cocoon sock yarn #4, #6 and #3 (70 percent wool/30 percent nylon) from Plymouth Yarn Co.

Harris Tweed Rib Socks

Design by Edie Eckman

Skill Level

■■■□ INTERMEDIATE

Size
Man's

Finished Measurements
Foot Circumference: 8 inches
Foot Length: 11 inches

Materials
- Sock weight superwash merino wool/ nylon blend yarn (192 yds/50g per ball): 2 balls brown/gray tweed
- Size 2 (2.75mm) knitting needles or size needed to obtain gauge: double-pointed OR 2 circular OR 1 long circular
- Stitch markers
- Tapestry needle

Gauge
15 sts and 20 rnds = 2 inches in St st.
To save time, take time to check gauge.

Pattern Stitch
Harris Tweed Rib (multiple of 4 sts)
Rnds 1 and 2: *K1, p2, k1; rep from * around.
Rnds 3 and 4: Purl around.
Rnds 5 and 6: Rep Rows 1 and 2.
Rnds 7 and 8: Knit around.
Rep Rnds 1–8 for pat.

Pattern Note
Refer to Basic Sock pattern on page 4 for specifics of arranging stitches on needles according to your preferred method of knitting.

Sock

Cuff
Cast on 56 sts loosely.

Arrange sts for working in the rnd. Join, being careful not to twist sts. Work in Harris Tweed Rib pat until sock measures 6½ inches from beg.

Heel
Slip next 26 sts onto 2 needles (for double-pointed needles method), 1 needle (for 2 circular needles method) or one half of needle (for long circular needle method) for instep. Work back and forth in rows on rem 30 sts for heel flap as follows:

Row 1 (WS): K2, purl to last 2 sts, k2. Turn.

Row 2 (RS): Knit. Turn.

Rep [Rows 1 and 2] 13 times, ending with a RS row.

Turning heel
Note: Sl 1 as to knit on RS rows and sl 1 as to purl on WS rows.

Row 1 (WS): P17, p2tog, p1. Turn, leaving rem sts unworked.

Row 2 (RS): Sl 1, k5, ssk, k1, turn.

Row 3: Sl 1, p6, p2tog, p1, turn.

Row 4: Sl 1, k7, ssk, k1, turn.

Row 5: Sl 1, p8, p2tog, p1, turn.

Row 6: Sl 1, k9, ssk, k1, turn.

Row 7: Sl 1, p10, p2tog, p1, turn.

Row 8: Sl 1, k11, ssk, k1, turn.

Row 9: Sl 1, p12, p2tog, p1, turn.

Row 10: Sl 1, k13, ssk, k1, turn.

Row 11: Sl 1, p14, p2tog, p1, turn.

Row 12: Sl 1, k15, ssk, k1, turn.

Row 13: Sl 1, p15, p2tog.

Row 14: Sl 1, k14, ssk—16 sts.

Gusset

Rnd 1: With RS of heel facing you, pick up and knit 15 sts along right edge of heel flap; knit 26 instep sts; pick up and knit 15 sts along left edge of heel flap, knit first 8 sts of heel—72 sts.

Rnd 2: On right edge of heel flap, knit to 4 sts from end of gusset sts, k2tog, k2; knit instep sts; on left edge of heel flap, k2, ssk, knit to end of rnd—70 sts.

Rnd 3: Knit around.

Rep [Rnds 2 and 3] 7 times—56 sts.

Foot

Work even until foot measures 9 inches from back of heel, or about 2 inches shorter than desired length of sock. Move markers (or move instep sts) so 1 bottom-of-foot st on each side moves to instep sts/needle—28 instep sts and 28 bottom-of-foot sts.

Toe shaping

Rnd 1: Knit to 3 sts before right edge of foot, k2tog, k1; on instep, k1, ssk, knit to 3 sts before left edge of foot, k2tog, k1; on bottom of foot, k1, ssk, knit to end of in rnd—52 sts.

Rnd 2: Knit around.

Rep [Rnds 1 and 2] 6 times—28 sts.

Work [Rnd 1 only] 3 times—16 sts.

Knit first 4 sts of next rnd and arrange sts so that 8 sts for the top of the foot are on 1 needle and 8 sts for the bottom of the foot are on a 2nd needle.

Finishing

With tapestry needle, graft toe tog. Weave in all ends. ❖

Sample knit with Happy Feet #3 (90 percent superwash merino wool/10 percent nylon) from Plymouth Yarn Co.

Baby Lace Socks

Design by Edie Eckman

Skill Level

■■■□ INTERMEDIATE

Sizes

6–12 months (18–24 months) Instructions are given for smallest size, with larger size in parentheses. When only one number is given, it applies to both sizes.

Finished Measurements

Foot Circumference: 6½ inches
Foot Length: 3¾ (4¼) inches

Materials

- DK weight baby alpaca yarn (125 yds/50g per ball): 1 ball lavender
- Size 3 (3.25mm) knitting needles or size needed to obtain gauge: double-pointed OR 2 circular OR 1 long circular
- Split-ring stitch markers
- Tapestry needle

Gauge

14 sts and 16 rnds = 2 inches/5mm in St st.
To save time, take time to check gauge.

Pattern Note

Refer to Basic Sock pattern on page 4 for specifics of arranging stitches on needles according to your preferred method of knitting.

Sock

Cuff

Cast on 32 sts loosely.

Arrange sts for working in the rnd. Join, being careful not to twist sts.

Knit 1 rnd.

Next rnd: *K1, p1; rep from * around.

Rep last rnd until cuff measures 1 inch.

Ankle

Rnds 1–3: Knit.

Rnd 4: *K5, yo, sl 1 as to knit, k2tog, psso; yo; rep from * around.

Rnd 5: Knit.

Rnd 6: *K6, yo, ssk; rep from * around.

Rnds 7 and 8: Knit.

Rnd 9: K1, *yo, sl 1 as to knit, k2tog, psso; yo, k5; rep from * twice more; yo, sl 1 as to knit, k2tog, psso; yo, k4.

Rnd 10: Knit.

Rnd 11: K2; *yo, ssk; k6; rep from * twice more; yo, ssk, k4.

Rnds 12 and 13: Knit.

Heel

K16 sts. Turn.

Arrange sts for working heel, with 16 sts on heel flap and 16 sts on instep. Work next rows back and forth on heel sts only.

Row 1 (WS): Sl 1 as to purl, purl across. Turn.

Row 2 (RS): Sl 1 as to knit, knit across. Turn.

Rep [Rows 1 and 2] 7 more times, ending with a RS row.

Turning heel

Note: Sl 1 as to knit on RS rows and sl 1 as to purl on WS rows.

Row 1 (WS): P10, p2tog, p1. Turn, leaving rem sts unworked.

Row 2 (RS): Sl 1, k5, ssk, k1, turn.

Row 3: Sl 1, p6, p2tog, p1, turn.

Row 4: Sl 1, k7, ssk, k1, turn.

Baby Lace Socks

Design by Edie Eckman

Skill Level

 ◼◼◼◻ INTERMEDIATE

Sizes

6–12 months (18–24 months) Instructions are given for smallest size, with larger size in parentheses. When only one number is given, it applies to both sizes.

Finished Measurements

Foot Circumference: 6½ inches
Foot Length: 3¾ (4¼) inches

Materials

- DK weight baby alpaca yarn (125 yds/50g per ball): 1 ball lavender
- Size 3 (3.25mm) knitting needles or size needed to obtain gauge: double-pointed OR 2 circular OR 1 long circular
- Split-ring stitch markers
- Tapestry needle

3 LIGHT

Gauge

14 sts and 16 rnds = 2 inches/5mm in St st.
To save time, take time to check gauge.

Pattern Note

Refer to Basic Sock pattern on page 4 for specifics of arranging stitches on needles according to your preferred method of knitting.

Sock

Cuff

Cast on 32 sts loosely.

Arrange sts for working in the rnd. Join, being careful not to twist sts.

Knit 1 rnd.

Next rnd: *K1, p1; rep from * around.

Rep last rnd until cuff measures 1 inch.

Ankle

Rnds 1–3: Knit.

Rnd 4: *K5, yo, sl 1 as to knit, k2tog, psso; yo; rep from * around.

Rnd 5: Knit.

Rnd 6: *K6, yo, ssk; rep from * around.

Rnds 7 and 8: Knit.

Rnd 9: K1, *yo, sl 1 as to knit, k2tog, psso; yo, k5; rep from * twice more; yo, sl 1 as to knit, k2tog, psso; yo, k4.

Rnd 10: Knit.

Rnd 11: K2; *yo, ssk; k6; rep from * twice more; yo, ssk, k4.

Rnds 12 and 13: Knit.

Heel

K16 sts. Turn.

Arrange sts for working heel, with 16 sts on heel flap and 16 sts on instep. Work next rows back and forth on heel sts only.

Row 1 (WS): Sl 1 as to purl, purl across. Turn.

Row 2 (RS): Sl 1 as to knit, knit across. Turn.

Rep [Rows 1 and 2] 7 more times, ending with a RS row.

Turning heel

Note: *Sl 1 as to knit on RS rows and sl 1 as to purl on WS rows.*

Row 1 (WS): P10, p2tog, p1. Turn, leaving rem sts unworked.

Row 2 (RS): Sl 1, k5, ssk, k1, turn.

Row 3: Sl 1, p6, p2tog, p1, turn.

Row 4: Sl 1, k7, ssk, k1, turn.

Row 5: Sl 1, p8, p2tog, turn.

Row 6: Sl 1, k8, ssk—10 sts.

Gusset

Rnd 1: With RS of heel facing you, pick up and knit 8 sts along right edge of heel flap, knit 16 instep sts, pick up and knit 8 sts along left edge of heel flap, knit first 5 sts of heel—42 sts.

Rnd 2: On right edge of heel flap, knit to 3 sts from end of gusset sts, k2tog, k1; knit instep sts; on left edge of heel flap, k1, ssk, knit rem sts in rnd—40 sts.

Rnd 3: Knit.

Rep [Rnds 2 and 3] 4 times—32 sts.

Foot

Work even until foot measures 2¾ (3¼) inches from back of heel.

Toe shaping

Rnd 1: Knit to 3 sts before right edge of foot, k2tog, k1; k1, ssk, knit to 3 sts before left edge of foot, k2tog, k1; k1, ssk, knit to end of in rnd—28 sts.

Rnd 2: Knit.

Rep [Rnds 1 and 2] 3 times—16 sts.

Rep Rnd 1—12 sts.

Finishing

Arrange sts so that 6 sts for the top of the foot are on 1 needle, and 6 sts for the bottom of the foot are on a 2nd needle.

With tapestry needle, graft toe tog. Weave in all ends. ❖

Sample knit with Baby Alpaca DK yarn #1720 (100 percent baby alpaca) from Plymouth Yarn Co.

General Information

Inches into Millimeters & Centimeters

All measurements are rounded off slightly.

inches	mm	cm	inches	cm	inches	cm	inches	cm	inches	cm
⅛	3	0.3	3	7.5	13	33.0	26	66.0	39	99.0
¼	6	0.6	3½	9.0	14	35.5	27	68.5	40	101.5
⅜	10	1.0	4	10.0	15	38.0	28	71.0	41	104.0
½	13	1.3	4½	11.5	16	40.5	29	73.5	42	106.5
⅝	15	1.5	5	12.5	17	43.0	30	76.0	43	109.0
¾	20	2.0	5½	14	18	46.0	31	79.0	44	112.0
⅞	22	2.2	6	15.0	19	48.5	32	81.5	45	114.5
1	25	2.5	7	18.0	20	51.0	33	84.0	46	117.0
1¼	32	3.8	8	20.5	21	53.5	34	86.5	47	119.5
1½	38	3.8	9	23.0	22	56.0	35	89.0	48	122.0
1¾	45	4.5	10	25.5	23	58.5	36	91.5	49	124.5
2	50	5.0	11	28.0	24	61.0	37	94.0	50	127.0
2½	65	6.5	12	30.5	25	63.5	38	96.5		

Glossary

bind off—used to finish an edge

cast on—process of making foundation stitches used in knitting

decrease—means of reducing the number of stitches in a row

increase—means of adding to the number of stitches in a row

intarsia—method of knitting a multicolored pattern into the fabric

knitwise—insert needle into stitch as if to knit

long tail cast on—method of cast-on where length of yarn about an inch long for each stitch is left at end before making first cast-on stitch

make 1—method of increasing using the strand between the last stitch worked and the next stitch

place marker—placing a purchased marker or loop of contrasting yarn onto the needle for ease in working a pattern repeat

purlwise—insert needle into stitch as if to purl

right side—side of garment or piece that will be seen when worn

selvage stitch—edge stitch used to make seaming easier

slip, slip, knit—method of decreasing by moving stitches from left needle to right needle and working them together

slip stitch—an unworked stitch slipped from left needle to right needle, usually as if to purl

work even—continue to work in the pattern as established without working any increases or decreases

work in pattern as established—continue to work following the pattern stitch as it has been set up or established on the needle, working any increases or decreases in such a way that the established pattern remains the same

yarn over—method of increasing by wrapping the yarn over the right needle without working a stitch

House of White Birches, Berne, Indiana 46711 DRGnetwork.com

Abbreviations & Symbols

approx	approximately
beg	begin/beginning
CC	contrasting color
ch	chain stitch
cm	centimeter(s)
cn	cable needle
dec	decrease/decreases/decreasing
dpn(s)	double-pointed needle(s)
g	gram
inc	increase/increases/increasing
k	knit
k2tog	knit 2 stitches together
LH	left hand
lp(s)	loop(s)
m	meter(s)
M1	make one stitch
MC	main color
mm	millimeter(s)
oz	ounce(s)
p	purl

pat(s)	pattern(s)
p2tog	purl 2 stitches together
psso	pass slipped stitch over
p2sso	pass 2 slipped stitches over
rem	remain/remaining
rep	repeat(s)
rev St st	reverse stockinette stitch
RH	right hand
rnd(s)	rounds
RS	right side
skp	slip 1, knit 1, pass slipped stitch over—one stitch decreased
sk2p	slip 1, knit 2 together, pass slipped stitch over—2 stitches have been decreased
sl	slip
sl 1k	slip 1 knitwise
sl 1p	slip 1 purlwise
sl st	slip stitch(es)
ssk	slip, slip, knit these 2 stitches together—a decrease
st(s)	stitch(es)

St st	stockinette stitch/stocking stitch
tbl	through back loop(s)
tog	together
WS	wrong side
wyib	with yarn in back
wyif	with yarn in front
yd(s)	yard(s)
yfwd	yarn forward
yo	yarn over

[ ] work instructions within brackets as many times as directed

( ) work instructions within parentheses in the place directed

** repeat instructions following the asterisks as directed

* repeat instructions following the single asterisk as directed

" inch(es)

Standard Yarn Weight System
Categories of yarn, gauge ranges, and recommended needle sizes

Yarn Weight Symbol & Category Names	1 SUPER FINE	2 FINE	3 LIGHT	4 MEDIUM	5 BULKY	6 SUPER BULKY
Type of Yarns in Category	Sock, Fingering, Baby	Sport, Baby	DK, Light Worsted	Worsted, Afghan, Aran	Chunky, Craft, Rug	Bulky, Roving
Knit Gauge Range* in Stockinette Stitch to 4 inches	27–32 sts	23–26 sts	21–24 sts	16–20 sts	12–15 sts	6–11 sts
Recommended Needle in Metric Size Range	2.25–3.25mm	3.25–3.75mm	3.75–4.5mm	4.5–5.5mm	5.5–8mm	8mm and larger
Recommended Needle U.S. Size Range	1 to 3	3 to 5	5 to 7	7 to 9	9 to 11	11 and larger

* **GUIDELINES ONLY:** The above reflect the most commonly used gauges and needle sizes for specific yarn categories.

How to Check Gauge

A correct stitch gauge is very important. Please take the time to work a stitch gauge swatch about 4 x 4 inches. Measure the swatch. If the number of stitches and rows are fewer than indicated under "Gauge" in the pattern, your needles are too large. Try another swatch with smaller-size needles. If the number of stitches and rows are more than indicated under "Gauge" in the pattern, your needles are too small. Try another swatch with larger-size needles.

Skill Levels

BEGINNER

Beginner projects for first-time knitters using basic stitches. Minimal shaping.

EASY

Easy projects using basic stitches, repetitive stitch patterns, simple color changes and simple shaping and finishing.

INTERMEDIATE

Intermediate projects with a variety of stitches, mid-level shaping and finishing.

EXPERIENCED

Experienced projects using advanced techniques and stitches, detailed shaping and refined finishing.

Knitting Needle Conversion Chart

U.S.	1	2	3	4	5	6	7	8	9	10	10½	11	13	15	17	19	35	50
Continental-mm	2.25	2.75	3.25	3.5	3.75	4	4.5	5	5.5	6	6.5	8	9	10	12.75	15	19	25

House of White Birches, Berne, Indiana 46711   DRGnetwork.com

Kitchener Stitch

This method of weaving with two needles is used for the toes of socks and flat seams. To weave the edges together and form an unbroken line of stockinette stitch, divide all stitches evenly onto two knitting needles—one behind the other. Thread yarn into tapestry needle. Hold needles with wrong sides together and work from right to left as follows:

Step 1: Insert tapestry needle into first stitch on front needle as to purl. Draw yarn through stitch, leaving stitch on knitting needle.

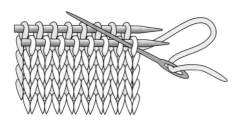

Step 2: Insert tapestry needle into the first stitch on the back needle as to purl. Draw yarn through stitch and slip stitch off knitting needle.

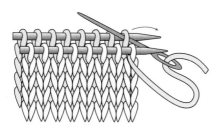

Step 3: Insert tapestry needle into the next stitch on same (back) needle as to knit, leaving stitch on knitting needle.

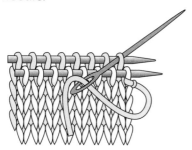

Step 4: Insert tapestry needle into the first stitch on the front needle as to knit. Draw yarn through stitch and slip stitch off knitting needle.

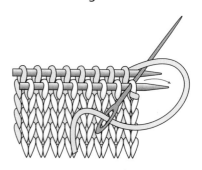

Step 5: Insert tapestry needle into the next stitch on same (front) needle as to purl. Draw yarn through stitch, leaving stitch on knitting needle.

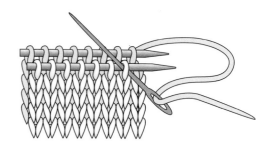

Repeat Steps 2 through 5 until one stitch is left on each needle. Then repeat Steps 2 and 4. Fasten off. Woven stitches should be the same size as adjacent knitted stitches.

Meet the Designer

Designer Edie Eckman has her hands in many aspects of the fiber arts—teaching, writing, designing and editing. Her designs are contemporary classics accessible to the average knitter or crocheter and they have appeared in many yarn company publications, magazines and pattern leaflets. Edie travels extensively to teach at conventions, shops and guilds.

She is the author of numerous ASN publications, such as *Learn to Knit Cables*, *Knit a Dozen Beanies* and *Learn to Knit Socks*. She is also the author of *The Crochet Answer Book* and *Beyond the Square Crochet Motifs* (Storey Publishing).

Edie grew up in Georgia and learned to knit literally at the knee of her live-in grandmother. She now lives in the Shenandoah Valley of Virginia with her husband, two children, a dog and a vast yarn stash.

The Next Step

Now that you've mastered new sock-knitting techniques, try working two socks at a time on circular needles, using separate balls of yarn for each sock.

Acknowledgements

The author would like to acknowledge the many knitters who have experimented with and popularized modern sock knitting, most particularly Cat Bordhi, whose amazing ability to think outside the box astounds me. Thanks, too, to Alicia Morse and Claudia Wittmann for their accurate and speedy sample knitting.

E-mail: Customer_Service@whitebirches.com

HOUSE of WHITE BIRCHES
PUBLISHERS SINCE 1947

How to Knit Socks: Three Methods Made Easy is published by DRG, 306 East Parr Road, Berne, IN 46711, telephone (260) 589-4000. Printed in USA. Copyright © 2008 DRG. All rights reserved. This publication may not be reproduced in part or in whole without written permission from the publisher.

RETAIL STORES: If you would like to carry this pattern book or any other DRG publications, call the Wholesale Department at Annie's Attic to set up a direct account: (903) 636-4303. Also, request a complete listing of publications available from DRG.

Every effort has been made to ensure that the instructions in this pattern book are complete and accurate. We cannot, however, take responsibility for human error, typographical mistakes or variations in individual work.

STAFF

Editor: Jeanne Stauffer
Managing Editor: Dianne Schmidt
Technical Editor: Kathy Wesley
Copy Supervisor: Michelle Beck
Copy Editors: Amanda Ladig, Mary O'Donnell
Graphic Arts Supervisor: Ronda Bechinski

Graphic Artist: Jessi Butler
Art Director: Brad Snow
Assistant Art Director: Nick Pierce
Photography Supervisor: Tammy Christian
Photography: Matt Owen
Photo Stylist: Tammy Steiner

ISBN: 978-1-59217-235-1

3 4 5 6 7 8 9

House of White Birches, Berne, Indiana 46711   DRGnetwork.com

18

21

24

28

32

36

40